ARE THERE ANY ANSWERS?

Clark H. Pinnock

DIMENSION BOOKS

BETHANY FELLOWSHIP, INC.
Minneapolis, Minnesota

Are There Any Answers?
by Clark H. Pinnock

ISBN 0-87123-009-7

Copyright © 1972
The Moody Bible Institute
of Chicago

Published in 1976 by

DIMENSION BOOKS
Bethany Fellowship, Inc.
6820 Auto Club Road
Minneapolis, Minnesota 55438

Printed in the United States of America

Contents

Preface

CONSIDER TWO QUESTIONS which are of paramount importance for the human situation and cannot be easily sidestepped:

1. How are we as modern men going to be able to cope with our dilemmas which seem so humanly insoluble?

2. Is there a resource from beyond the human situation which can both ease the predicament and make good its own truth claim?

The crisis in human values today makes these questions urgent. Man's dignity and worth are in doubt, and the foundations of meaningful existence have been severely shaken. Is there a solution outside of man and beyond his present possibilities which can make sense of life as it is lived out? If this solution can distinguish itself as true amid the welter of conflicting truth claims, then the discovery of it would be the most valuable event in our lives.

In no sense is the reader asked to accept Christian answers to these questions blindly. To demand that would be both immoral and futile. The reader is only asked to consider how this viewpoint was reached.

Why should the Christian faith get a hearing at all? Simply because any person who is serious about discovering truth, especially truth of cosmic significance, is already committed to expending great effort in that quest. If one supposed that a bomb had been planted in a building, unless he were a fool he would insist on fleeing that place and demand that a thorough search of it be made before he reentered.

If the Christian faith is true, it is the clue to everything there is and the secret to human fulfillment in this world and the next. So the stakes are high. This is no time for empty-headed indifference. The mere *possibility* that the message of the Bible is true is ample reason for reading this pamphlet through!

Right now you may not be a believer in God. Even after you read this essay you may be of the same mind. The worst you can do is to evade these two questions. While truth passes by on the other side, you could look away, pretending not to notice. Yet, an ostrich with its head in the sand deserves little admiration.

Answers to the fundamental questions of human life are very few these days. A current of uneasiness and futility pervades our culture. Though we have witnessed great advances in scientific knowledge and control, we have also experienced deep doubt concerning the goodness and meaning of life. Still, plenty of people do go through life without seriously considering the claims of Christ. At least do that. You have nothing to lose and plenty to gain.

1

The Human Predicament

ANYONE ALIVE to the mood of our culture can hardly fail to notice a current of uneasiness and futility running through our philosophy, literature, and drama. The real revolution in our day has less to do with sex, drugs, or politics than with the crisis in human values. An uneasy restlessness has arisen as the meaning and purpose of life has become obscure and hidden. How is man to cope with existence on the basis of no more than faith in himself?

In a recent interview, I. F. Stone admitted,

> I feel more and more ignorant, because I don't have any answers anymore. It's pretty awful to run a publication that's supposed to supply people with answers and not have any answers. It's therapeutic for me, but I don't know whether it does anybody else any good or not.[1]

Or listen to Professor Donald Kalish of the philosophy department of UCLA,

> There is no system of philosophy to spin out. There are no ethical truths, there are just clarifications of particular ethical problems. Take advantage of these clarifications and work out your own existence. You are mistaken to think that anyone ever had the answers. There are no answers. Be brave and face up to it.[2]

The Metaphysical Problem

Such admissions are tragic because, as Ionesco put it, "Cut off from his religious, metaphysical and transcendental roots, man is lost; all his actions become senseless, absurd, useless."[3] The ground has been cut away from beneath the meaningfulness of human life. Man has no basis for affirming the value or direction of existence.

Waiting for Godot is the play for our time. Man *is* just waiting around!

Beckett puts the value of man and his culture at zero and conforms his style to his theme. James Joyce, Beckett's friend, said of his work, "Here is life without God—just look at it."

Life is in many ways a secular wasteland. "It is a tale told by an idiot, full of sound and fury, signifying nothing" (Shakespeare, *Macbeth*).

The problem runs very deep. Toward the end of his life, Theodore Dreiser confessed,

> As I see him, the unutterably infinitesimal individual weaves among the mysteries a floss-like and wholly meaningless course—if course it be. In short, I catch no meaning from all I have seen, and pass quite as I came, confused and dismayed.[4]

Similarly, Bertrand Russell's famous lines bear repeating.

> That man is the product of causes which had no prevision of the end they were achieving; that his origin, his growth, his hopes and fears, his loves and beliefs, are but the outcome of accidental collocations of atoms; that no fire, no heroism, no intensity of thought and feeling, can preserve an individual life beyond the grave; that all the labour of the ages, all the devotion, all the inspiration, all the noonday brightness of human genius, are destined to extinction in the vast death of the solar system, and that the whole temple of man's achievement must inevitably be buried beneath the debris of a universe in ruins—all these things, if not quite beyond dispute, are yet so nearly certain, that no philosophy which

rejects them can hope to stand. Only within the scaffolding of these truths, only on the firm foundation of unyielding despair, can the soul's habitation henceforth be safely built. [5]

Russell makes it very difficult for a person who shares his secular point of view to escape from the inexorable logic of his argument. How does one cope with the pointlessness of it all?

A case in point comes up in the conclusion to archeologist Geoffrey Bibbey's book, *Looking for Dilmun*. In the body of this scholarly work, Bibbey gives an interesting account of a great ancient civilization, beginning about 3,000 B.C. and dying about 1,000 B.C. whose name was even unknown to us for two millennia. Then he concludes,

> And when, one day, it will all have been said and done, when the last basketful of earth has been carried up from the diggings, and the last word of the last report written—*what will it all have mattered?*[6]

What indeed? What does all of human history mean? And if it means nothing when it is dead and gone, then what does it mean when it is alive and in progress? The problem of meaninglessness is not easily solved. Its logic seems intrinsic and inescapable.

Albert Camus was able to see that the nature of the problem was theological.

> Up 'til now man derived his coherence from his Creator. But from the moment that he consecrates his rupture with him, he finds himself delivered over to the fleeting moment and to wasted sensibility.[7]

Friedrich Nietzsche saw what was coming in the wake of man's turning away from God.

> Is there still an up and down? Are we not wandering aimlessly through an infinite void? Does not an empty space breathe upon us? Has it not grown colder?[8]

At first, freedom from God seems to be an exhilarating release. It soon proves to be frightening. For what good is freedom in a universe infected with absurdity? What significance has any choice man may decide to make? Deep ambiguity lies at the heart of everything, and our lives are ruled by senseless fate.

Edmund Fuller remarked,

> Our present generation now practising the art of fiction is the first generation in which there have been large, influential, and

admired groups of novelists working, in many instances quite unconsciously, on the tacit or declared premise that there is no God, basing the patterns of their work on the implications, again often unconscious, that arise out of that premise.[9]

These implications are often quite grim. In part they account for the shallow superficiality of modern culture. Camus dryly remarked,

A single sentence will suffice for modern man: he fornicated and read the papers. After that vigorous definition, the subject will be, if I may say so, exhausted.[10]

Not so much *should* people have a clearer understanding of life's basis, but sooner or later they will *have* to.

The shape of man's predicament is vividly and concretely symbolized by death. For Sartre, death is the final absurdity which fittingly finishes off what the absurdity of birth began. Death is the "nihilation" of all man's possibilities. All of the existentialist philosophers insist that learning how to die properly is essential. But how precisely does one learn to do that? In death we come so dramatically to the end of human resources. The expectation of it creates a melancholia which will not be soothed unless death itself is defeated.

THE MORAL PROBLEM

So far we have considered only the metaphysical problem man faces: that he cannot find the meaning of his life on the basis of secular assumptions. But a moral side to the human predicament is no less intractable for this point of view. If recent history has taught us anything, it is that man's deepest problems lie within *himself*. Those philosophies which paint a rosy future for man's unaided progress are far removed from empirical reality. William Golding has done us a fine service by his X ray of man's moral condition in *Lord of the Flies*. He uncovered in that novel the deeply rooted malice which lurks in the heart of every man. The basic problem today is man, enslaved to his own self-centered nature, and the feelings of lust, greed, jealousy, and pride which well up within his being. Better education and laws will not solve this problem. Man himself has to be changed.

The very fact of human savagery and narcissism caused nineteenth century liberalism to stumble and fall. As C. E. M. Joad admitted,

> It is because we rejected the doctrine of original sin that we on the left were always being disappointed; disappointed by the refusal of people to be reasonable, by the subservience of intellect to emotion, by the failure of true socialism to arrive.[11]

Langdon Gilkey had his youthful optimism about human nature knocked out of him during his incarceration in a Japanese prisoner of war camp in northern China during the Second World War. He found to his dismay that, when the niceties of civilized convention were removed and all but the bare essentials stripped away, the reality of man's self-seeking and moral perversity rushed to the surface with distressing clarity.[12] This lesson was also forcibly taught by the Russian novelist Dostoevski when he placed his searchlight on the stubborn irrationality and impulse of destructiveness in man.

Supposed Solutions

Is technology the solution to man's problems? Sigmund Freud, a man so sensitive to one kind of illusion, fell prey to another when he declared his faith in omnicompetent science to bring in the age of gold. Ironical it is that the Nazis, acting on Freud's own materialistic and deterministic principles, should have ejected him from Austria and sent him packing to Britain for refuge. Science has done much for mankind, but it has *not* made us good!

Technology provides man with the power to control nature and to turn its potential to his uses. But it says nothing about what those uses shall be. Science is impotent to help us, because it succeeds only in making a bad man better at being bad. The discoveries of science are made in the innocency of the laboratory. But they are applied by men immersed in the murky realm of human history. Technology then does not solve our problem. It only makes a solution more urgent than ever.

A strident cry for political revolution comes from many sides today. Man's moral predicament injects a note of irony into the whole movement in three respects.

1. What is there to bind us in sacred solidarity to our human kind? Moral passion seems to be out of place in a universe devoid of God. There is really nothing to live or die for.

2. Which revolution shall we identify with? Secular man is caught in a paralyzing relativism in which his values are immersed in the flux of history. "Whirl is king, having cast

out Zeus" (Aristophanes). A person is not able to transcend his finite perspective and decide which political or social program deserves his commitment.

3. Granted, there are inequities in the "system." Was there ever a human order in which this was not true? In the last analysis, neither racism nor war nor pollution is the deepest problem but rather *man* himself. Modifying the system will not deal with hate and self-centeredness and greed. Something more is needed.

Andy Warhol, asked about his six-hour film which shows a man sleeping, commented, "It keeps you from thinking. I wish I were a machine."

Alongside the problem of outer space—man alone in an impersonal universe—is the problem of inner space. People today are feeling an emptiness inside. Drugs came along at an expedient time, and thousands sought answers there. But disenchantment has started to set in. Drugs do not deliver love and peace. They only mess you up without changing you on the inside. But one thing is clear. Drugs are a symptom of deep inward need. Until people are given something better for that problem, they are going to go on using them.

What does this all add up to? Analysis does not solve anything. Unmasking the human predicament in no way contributes to its resolution. What it does is drive us in the direction of seeking for answers. Apparently, modern man is in deep trouble trying to establish a framework in which to live out his existence; he has achieved scant success. The burning question now is, "Are other resources available to us which can enable us again to make a joyful affirmation of life and to resolve the moral problem?"

2

A Word from the Outside

MAN STANDS IN NEED of an *axiology* (set of values) which can satisfy his deepest needs and hunger. But before one can be put forth, it is imperative to face the truth question. Conceivably, a religion or philosophy might be internally consistent, its values profoundly satisfying, and still be completely false and illusory. Correspondence of any such axiology with the real world has to be established. Values are not self-validating; they need to be grounded in solid fact.

Later on, we will show how the Christian faith can supply a series of answers to the human predicament nothing short of sensational. Before that, the objective evidence of the truthfulness of the Christian message should be considered.

Many people think that Christianity deals in intangibles and is unwilling to submit its claims to any kind of test or verification. On the contrary, the Christian faith is for the tough-minded. Its claim rests upon accessible data derived from the empirical realm. Christians believe that factual reality, as investigated by the impartial observer, points to the truth of their faith. Therefore, it is an ideal religion to examine, since most competitors beg the truth question altogether and will not submit to critical examination.

ANTECEDENT PROBABILITY

A Christian is a person who is convinced that the fact of Christ is the plainest clue to the meaning of things. He believes that God Himself has confronted us in Him in the factual realm. Before going into the reasons why Christians think this way, let us consider several questions.

Why is it that human beings are addicted to a propensity for order? Why do we live our lives and raise our children on the premise, tacit or otherwise, that reality is ultimately purposive and makes sense? Why is it that the word "ought" springs so easily to our lips? How did the ethical category arise out of a world consisting, we are told, only of material atoms? If the Nazis "should have known better," *why* should they? If their actions were damnable, before what tribunal? Why is there "something" rather than "nothing"? And more especially, why this enormously complex and fascinating "something"? Why is it that so many who turn away from God end up in despair? (Voltaire cried out, "I wish I had never been born.") Do fish complain that the sea is wet? Is it possible that the desire which no earthly thing can seem to satisfy calls for another kind of nourishment? C. S. Lewis remarked, "If I find in myself a desire which no experience in this world can satisfy, the most probable explanation is that I was made for another world."[1]

These questions, and many more like them, direct us to situations in our immediate experience which are "odd" and set us thinking along the right lines. They raise the ultimate religious questions about our life. They create a kind of "antecedent probability" which suggests that the New Testament claims might just be true after all.

THE FACT OF CHRIST

The hub of the Christian message is the public revelation in Jesus of Nazareth. The first apostles set forth no philosophical system. They made a factual announcement. In Jesus Christ there came into the world a living Redeemer and absolute truth itself. This fact was of paramount importance to the human race.

As a matter of interest, the world into which Christ came was very much like our own. Life was far from ideal. Men were sick of war. The moral fiber of society was weak. Religious skepticism abounded, accompanied by the fear of death and fate. The Christian message turned that world upside down (Acts 17:6), and Christians believe it could revolutionize our own. After all, as Chesterton once said, "Christianity has not been tried and found wanting; it has been found difficult and not tried."

·The point in the argument has now been reached in which the startling claim that God Himself has been incarnated in Jesus has to be justified in terms of historical evidence. By no means is it sufficient merely to assert that this is so. What kind of authenticating credentials exist to back up so grandiose a claim? We need to examine, first of all, the historical credibility of the New Testament records in which the claim appears.

We ask no one just to accept the New Testament documents a priori. Certain literary tests can be applied to writings of all kinds as a test of authenticity.[2] The first has to do with the history and state of the text. No document from ancient times is so well attested bibliographically. This is true because of the number and age of the manuscripts we possess. For example, the gap between the writing of Tacitus' Roman history and the oldest manuscript we possess of it is a full eight hundred years; then we have a total of only twenty good manuscripts. In contrast, we have thirteen thousand manuscript copies of portions of the New Testament, not counting abundant quotations of most of it in the church fathers. No parallel case of the age and number of manuscripts is as great as the New Testament.[3]

A second test is internal. The document under investigation must be permitted to declare its own intentions. If the document claims to be an eyewitness source, this is taken seriously, unless solid external evidence crops up to disqualify its claim. A sympathetic benefit of the doubt is given to the document if progress is to be made. Throughout the New Testament the writers put their material forward as firsthand testimony (Luke 1:1-4; 1 John 1:1-3).

Finally, confirmation from external data is highly desirable. A striking piece of this has come lately from a historian of Roman law, A. N. Sherwin-White. He undertook to examine the legal procedures recorded in the Gospels and Acts in the light of their Hellenistic and Roman background; he concluded on the basis of the study that the evidence for the historical reliability of the New Testament was overwhelming.[4]

Compare the situation in the Buddhist religion. Edward Conze, a scholar of Buddhism writes,

> A history of Buddhist thought might be expected to begin with an account of the teachings of the Buddha himself, or at least of the beliefs current in the most ancient community. The nature of our literary documents makes such an attempt fruitless and impossible.[5]

The furthest back one can penetrate is the legend of Buddha a couple of centuries after his death.[6]

The inescapable conclusion is that the cost of refusing to accredit the New Testament documents their historical reliability is complete historical skepticism. In order to avoid this unhappy conclusion, one must employ a critical skepticism so negative that were it applied to Napoleon Bonaparte, as it was by Richard Whately in his work, *Historic Doubts Relative to Napoleon Bonaparte*, it would cast doubt on his very existence!

THE CENTRAL FIGURE

A scant perusal of the New Testament material drives us to consider the central figure of every single book. Jesus Christ is a fact difficult to assimilate by one who has not yet decided to follow Him. His deep wisdom and flawless character have made a profound impression upon every generation.

Coincidentally, His teaching bristles with divine claims. He boldly undertakes to forgive sins; He demands unqualified obedience; He claims a unique relation with God His Father; He predicts His own resurrection and glorious return at the end of history. These claims, made by a mere man, would amount to imperial megalomania. Either Jesus is an imposter or mad, or else He is who He claimed to be. And few, when they have read the gospels, have concluded that Jesus was either imbalanced or deceitful.

C. S. Lewis sums up the real issue so clearly,

> I am trying here to prevent anyone saying the really foolish thing that people often say about him: "I'm ready to accept Jesus as a great moral teacher, but I don't accept his claim to be God." That is the one thing we must not say. A man who was merely a man and said the sort of things Jesus said would not be a great moral teacher. He would either be a lunatic—on the level with the man who says he is a poached egg—or else he would be the Devil of hell. You must make your choice. Either this man was, and is, the Son of God: or else a madman or something worse. You can shut him up for a fool, you can spit at him and kill him as a demon; or you can fall at his feet and call him Lord and God. But let us not come with any patronising nonsense about his being a great human teacher. He has not left that open to us. He did not intend to.[7]

We have to decide what to make of Him. A selflessness and genuine humility about Him cannot be missed. He certainly does not seem imbalanced or a crank. He literally gave His whole life in the service of others. Probably the safer recourse for a non-Christian is to ignore Him altogether. But as soon as He is considered, He is very difficult to evade.

The Resurrection

All of this stands alongside the most important piece of data—the bodily resurrection of Christ. Before His death, Jesus repeatedly staked the truth of His claim upon the fulfillment of His prediction that He would rise again. Later the apostles claimed that the authority and divinity of Jesus had been decisively validated by the fact of the resurrection (Acts 2:32; Romans 1:4). When he spoke at Athens, Paul told his skeptical audience that God had given them evidence for the truth of the gospel by raising up Christ from the dead (Acts 17:31). Clearly, the Christian faith rests upon a factually attested claim that death and sin have been conquered by Jesus. Here is a claim which can be examined, the importance of which demands investigation.

Jesus was put to death by crucifixion in the city of Jerusalem at the season of Passover. The place was teeming with people who were aware of Jesus' claims and what the issues were. Therefore, the officials in charge ordered a guard placed at Jesus' tomb to ensure that the body would not be removed and that a false rumor would not begin. Soon after, the disciples of Jesus, who had been dismayed and scattered by the trauma of the crucifixion, started to proclaim that Christ was risen. They did so in the very city where Jesus had died and with the tomb only minutes away. Here we have a historical situation in which the most likely hypothesis to explain the facts is the bodily resurrection of Christ!

Some have ventured to suggest that Jesus did not really die but escaped from the tomb and visited his forlorn disciples. This view makes the unlikely supposition that the Roman executioners did not know their business very well. Suppose that Jesus got out of the sealed tomb, eluded the guards, appeared to His disciples, and convinced them He was risen from the dead. This is a hypothesis for which there is no evidence and which is more difficult to believe than the resurrection itself.

Nor can we explain the empty tomb by attributing responsibility for the removal of the body to the foes of Jesus—Roman or Jewish. They had no motive for it. Their chief desire was to squelch the infant movement, not to contribute to its success. Nothing would have been easier, had they known where the body was, than for them to prick the balloon and expose the gospel as a fraud. But they did not. They did not because they could not.

Even less likely is the possibility that the disciples stole the body. Had they tried it, they would have been killed by the guard. Besides, events of the last week had shown Peter and his friends to be cowards in the face of danger. More important still, they may have been less than brave at first, but they were certainly not liars. Martyrs and hypocrites are not cut from the same cloth. That these men would expose themselves to death for a message they knew to be founded on a fabrication is not believable. Moreover, it collides with the righteousness of their ethic. The doctrine which the apostles preached was characterized by the highest ideals of integrity and honesty the world has yet heard. It makes no sense at all to charge them with foul conspiracy.

In addition to the evidence for the empty tomb, the New Testament records a series of appearances of Jesus to individuals and groups over a period of several weeks. These are described in some detail, and on one occasion involved five hundred people at one time. This series of appearances calls for some explanation. It certainly convinced the disciples that Jesus had conquered death and entered into a new mode of existence. Though afraid and discouraged prior to that time, they were changed by the appearances and took on an attitude of glorious certainty that Jesus was risen indeed. When the disciples came to realize the stupendous truth of the resurrection, they feared neither death nor social ostracism. Consequently, the Christian movement exploded across the Roman Empire and beyond. The history of that first century could not have been what it was were it not for the resurrection of Jesus. The Christian Messianic movement succeeded where others in that century did not, solely because of Christ's attested claim to have triumphed over death!

A Decision to Be Made

The evidence for the resurrection of Jesus is the kind that should be sufficient to incite belief in any ordinary matter of life. Verdicts have been reached in court cases on evidence not nearly so compelling. Thomas Arnold wrote,

> I have been used for many years to study the histories of other times, and to examine and weigh the evidence of those who have

31

written about them, and I know of no one fact in the history of mankind which is proved by better and fuller evidence of every sort, to the understanding of a fair inquirer, than the great sign which God has given us that Christ died and rose again from the dead.[8]

Frank Morrison, a lawyer, set out to disprove the resurrection of Jesus. The book would not be written; the stubbornness of the facts prevented it. Starting out with a bias against the resurrection, he was compelled by honesty to revise his presuppositions. The book he did write, *Who Moved the Stone?*, is a classic defense of the resurrection.

What value does evidence of this sort have? It gives grounds for our considering the New Testament message as a live option for our lives today. If Christ was raised, then all that He said was true. We are safe in believing His promises that in Him we can have peace with God and the forgiveness of our sins. All human decisions, whether legal or historical or related to daily life, are made on the basis of considerations such as these. Unbelief is often the result of ill-informed prejudice, and many who reject Christ do so without having examined the evidence for the gospel. This is an invitation to consider the fact of Christ and respond to it.

Before we move on, one thing ought to be clear. If Christianity is true, it deserves the commitment of an honest person, whether it will help him or not. Conversely, no one should believe this message unless it is true, however much it may offer to help him. The Christian faith is serious about its basis in truth. How rare this is! The very terms "religion" and "faith" in modern parlance have come to denote beliefs that are unsupported by factual evidence. Not so the Christian faith. It boldly seeks to win men's loyalty by appealing to their minds.

3

A Solid Footing

Now THAT WE HAVE SEEN how the Christian faith rests upon discoverable data in the real world, we may go on to explain how the human predicament may be solved by it. Coming into contact with the incarnation introduces us to a value system capable of yielding solid answers to man's dilemmas.

RELATIVISM

The first problem to be cleared up is that of relativism. How is man to arrive at ultimate truth from his finite perspective within the human situation? By himself he cannot. But Jesus Christ, in whom God acted in time/space history, tips us off to the nature of ultimate reality. Had He not come, how could we possibly transcend our cultural limitations and discover the real meaning of life and history? The Christian message is terribly exciting because it presents a solution which did not just bubble up out of the human situation, but comes to us from outside the flux of historical reality.

GROUND OF MEANING

One of the great illusions of recent secular thought has been the notion that one could empty out heaven without at the same time threatening the very foundations of earthly existence. In actual fact, a large part of the agony of modern man is *due* to his turning away from God. In doing that he has denied the only basis on which he might affirm the significance and value of anything, including himself. The dignity of man and the majesty of God are inextricably related. When a man or a culture dumps its faith in God, however distorted and weak that faith is, "business" does not continue "as usual." The whole vision of reality changes radically. The world is no longer held together by any unifying purpose. It is changed into a bare, alien, desolate universe of sense data and quantum mechanics. Man is subject to nature, but nature is indifferent to his needs. Man is free to choose, but what significance has any choice he makes in a world infected with absurdity? He is doomed to fight in vain against the myth of nothingness. When man loses God, he is nailed to a cross of despair from which there is no one to take him down. The Christian faith offers a ground of meaning which can truly sustain us.

COMPLETENESS

The root meaning of the Hebrew word for salvation is "enlargement" or "spaciousness." That is, it is the opposite of an unlovely, cramped, uncomfortable existence. Many people really think that faith in God is unworldly and opposed to a full human life. Nothing could be further from the truth. As C. S. Lewis said, "Because we love something else more than this world, we love even this world better than those who know no other." Later he wrote, "Aim at Heaven and you will get the earth 'thrown in'; aim at earth and you will get neither."[1]

The enemy of our souls gives empty promises. Only in Christ is found completeness (Colossians 2:10).

The Christian faith offers us a very high view of man and his possibilities. It directs us to the living God, who is personal and gracious. Our origins do not lie in a chance process. Rather we are related ontologically (because we exist) to our Maker and can be reconciled morally and spiritually to Him whom we have dishonored. As St. Augustine put it, "Thou hast formed us for thyself, and our hearts are restless till they find rest in thee."[2]

A condition for meaningful existence is that we relate ourselves to a dimension of significance beyond ourselves. This enables us to participate in reality that is intelligible and purposeful. In Christ we discover our true identity.

The Bible speaks of man's being in the "image of God." This phrase in the Old Testament describes man as the visible representative on earth of the invisible God. The "image" in ancient Near Eastern culture was a stand-in for the person depicted. The idea is that you and I have been appointed God's "vicars" (agents) on earth. All that we do in caring for this sacred trust and bringing forth the latent goodness of the earth, we can do for the glory of God and the good of our brothers. We can serve him precisely by "worldly" activity. No occupation is too mean nor skill too small but that it can be joyfully dedicated to God and bring fulfillment to us.

In recent years, the Marxist philosopher Ernst Bloch has been directing attention to the fundamental quality of hope in the human experience. But his thought lacks any clear explanation why one should believe mankind has something for which to hope.

The biblical faith affords us a sufficient reason and right to hope. Through Christ we enter into a relationship with the God who is sovereign over history and able to keep us in His love, come what may (Romans 8:28, 38-39). Far beyond the present, we know that God is directing history toward a glorious consummation. He gives us the promise of a world redeemed and renewed (2 Peter 3:13). All of this is not the vain projection of human dreams. Grounded in the resurrection of Jesus, His promise shatters our gloom and provides an unshakable foundation for our hope.

In our discussion of the human predicament earlier, we noted a moral dimension to the problem. The message of Jesus addresses itself precisely to that issue. The fundamental human problem is inside man himself—his insatiable greed and self-centeredness, his inhumanity to others, even those closest to him.

The solution is not better education, environmental control, or legal enactments, important as these all are. Man himself needs to be changed.

The Christian faith puts the moral problem in clear perspective. We have all gone astray from God (Isaiah 53:6); we keep falling short of his standards (Romans 3:23); if God gave us what we deserve, we would all be goners (Psalm 130:3). Deep inside of us we know something is seriously wrong. We are morally bankrupt and self-condemned even by the ideals we set for ourselves and hold sacred. The Bible has good news for us! God is gracious. He loves sinners and is seeking to draw them back to Himself. (Luke 15:3-32).

The major consequence of our sinful condition is alienation from God so that we are out of fellowship with Him. This accounts for much of our restlessness and soul-sorrow. So, the first thing God does is to offer us a full pardon through Christ. He takes the burden of responsibility for sin off of us (what unutterable relief!) and sets the vertical dimension right. "Therefore, being justified by faith, we have peace with God through our Lord Jesus Christ" (Romans 5:1).

He does this by means of the death of Jesus. In that act, God in Christ accepted the consequences of our sin and put us right with Himself (1 Peter 2:24). Becoming a Christian is a hard thing to do because it hurts to admit our own deeds are worthless and to stretch forth an empty hand to receive God's free gift. But we must do it, because salvation is only by grace (Ephesians 2:8-9), that is, unmerited favor of God.

But sin does more than to estrange us from God; it also enslaves us. We simply cannot set ourselves free from the inner perversity we sense. Not so much are we addicted to this or that, though that may be. The fact is that we are enslaved to a deep, inward corruption (John 8:34). We need a change of heart, and not only for our own sakes. The same self-destroying egoism also turns us against our brothers. But God does even more than liberate us. He also gives us a new nature (2 Corinthians 5:17); He enables us to love (Romans 5:5); He gives us the Holy Spirit to control us (Ephesians 5:18).

The rootlessness and unhappiness of modern man surely show that he does not have the resources within himself to achieve peace and fulfillment. In stark contrast to this dark frustration stands Christ's offer of deep and abiding joy. To all who come to Him, He promises rest of soul (Matthew 11:28-30), a peace that the world system cannot give (John 14:27), and a life which is truly abundant (John 10:10). Our anxiety is replaced with His ecstasy. He continually surprises us with joy. Let the psalmist express what we mean. "I waited patiently for the LORD; and he inclined unto me, and heard my cry. He brought me up also out of an horrible pit, out of the miry clay, and set my feet upon a rock, and established my goings. And he hath put a new song in my mouth, even praise unto our God: many shall see it, and fear, and shall trust in the LORD" (Psalm 40:1-3).

Singing and joy characterize biblical religion. "Fear not: for, behold, I bring you good tidings of great joy, which shall be to all people" (Luke 2:10). From man-centered thought comes only "despair in the place of hope, a miserable unceasing restlessness in place of peace, and either an ever-deepening sorrow or a chilling stoicism instead of true and abiding joy."[3] Whereas in Christ is found a peace that passes all understanding and a joy which the world system can neither give nor take away.

We are not arguing that the glorious fact of Christian experience is sufficient in and of itself to validate the truth of the Christian message. For religious experience alone, as William James has shown, is not capable of establishing either its source or its contents. But in its proper place, alongside the impressive fact of Christ and the ability of Christian truth to make sense of experienced reality, the existential encounter and relationship with Jesus seals our certitude and satisfies our longings.

4

Our Reasonable Faith

MODERN MAN stands in desperate need of answers to his existential dilemmas. This fact by itself does not tell us whether any such answers exist. It only creates the desire to search and see if they do.

A major problem in the quest after ultimate truth is the bewildering cacophony of contradictory and conflicting claims. They cannot all be true. How then do we tell them apart? Faith is, after all, a relational term. One always has faith *in* something. In that case, how is an object of faith that is proper to be distinguished from one that is not? If the pill one is about to swallow may be aspirin *or* arsenic, one should know well in advance which it is! Claims to truth need to be screened for their truth value.

Therefore in our discussion, we made no

arrogant demands that a person simply believe the gospel by blind faith. Such an approach not only would be calculated to fail and alienate any seeker after truth; it would also misrepresent the open-to-investigation form of the Christian message. God has revealed Himself in the public domain of human history. To that we have pointed the reader.

Have we asked for nothing by way of presuppositions then? A distinction needs to be made. There are presuppositions of *method*, and presuppositions of *content*. We have not asked that a person accept substantial conclusions of content in blind commitment. All we have asked is that the reader grant the existence of a real, factual world and the possibility of investigating it with positive results by the use of logic and empirical methods. Such a presupposition of method is the starting point in any science, and is valid if only because it has to be assumed to be refuted.

These are answers to the big questions that people ask. In Jesus Christ you can find a solid foundation on which to build your life. Evidence for the truth of the Christian message is evidence to which an honest man can subscribe with intellectual integrity. But God will not impose His gift of salvation upon anyone. We need to accept it if we are to possess it. The Bible depicts Christ standing before the door of the human heart, seeking an entrance (Revelation 3:20). We must individually (no one can do it for us) and deliberately (it is an act of our volition) invite Christ to be our Saviour and Lord. He wants to come in to bestow upon us the benefits of salvation and to become manager over our total being.

In "The Human Predicament," we described the secular life-style as incomparably bleak and empty. That was not the whole story. It does offer one tempting lure; it leaves a person lord of his own affairs and free to do exactly what he wants. If life has no meaning and no moral base, then there is no reason why one should not do only what is pleasurable and advantageous to himself.

A philosophy of meaninglessness can be the beginning of liberation. Christian commitment requires that we abandon autonomy. We need to bow twice. First, we must acknowledge that the God of the biblical revelation has the right to rule us and receive our total allegiance. Second, we have to confess our sin and guilt and call upon Christ to save us. God Himself promises that if we seek

Him in this way, we will find Him (Matthew 7:7).

Jesus never hid the fact from people that, although salvation was free, God demands total submission from His people. Many who wanted to follow Jesus in the enthusiasm of the moment were sent away by Him to consider the cost. "If anyone wishes to come after Me," He said, "let him deny himself, and take up his cross, and follow Me" (Mark 8:34). No one even superficially acquainted with Jesus' teachings could charge, as Marx did, that religion is the opiate of the people. On the contrary, Christian commitment is a demanding and serious business and should not be undertaken without careful consideration. It involves a renunciation of sin and self, and the willingness to let God take over complete control of the life.

Yet it is worth it all. Why not surrender your life to Jesus Christ? You stand to lose only a life which is empty, a life full of despair without Him. You stand to gain peace, pardon, and freedom in His presence. In relationship with Christ, to rephrase Macbeth, life becomes a tale told by Someone, signifying everything!

FOR FURTHER READING

Lewis, C. S. *Mere Christianity*. London: Fontana, 1955.

Pinnock, Clark H. *Set Forth Your Case*. Chicago: Moody, 1971.

Stott, John R. *Basic Christianity*. Grand Rapids: Eerdmans, 1958.

NOTES

CHAPTER 1

1. I. F. Stone, "With Atheists Like Him, Who Needs Believers?" *Christian Century*, Nov. 4, 1970, p. 1317.
2. Donald Kalish, "What (If Anything) to Expect from Today's Philosophers," *TIME*, Jan. 7, 1966, p. 24.
3. Cited in Martin Esslin, *Theatre of the Absurd* (New York: Doubleday, 1961), p. xix.
4. Theodore Dreiser, "What I Believe," *The Forum* 82(1929):320.
5. Bertrand Russell, *A Free Man's Worship* (Portland, Maine: Thomas Mosher, 1927), pp. 6-7.
6. Geoffrey Bibbey, *Looking for Dilmun* (New York: Knopf, 1970), p. 383.
7. Albert Camus, *The Rebel* (New York: Vintage Books, 1956), p. 47.
8. Friedrich Nietzsche, "The Gay Science," in *The Portable Nietzsche*, sect. 125, trans. and ed. Walter Kaufmann (New York: Viking Press, 1954), pp. 95-99.
9. Edmund Fuller, *Man in Modern Fiction* (New York: Random, 1958), p. 8.
10. Camus, *The Fall* (London: Penguin, 1957), p. 7.
11. C. E. M. Joad, *The Recovery of Belief* (London: Faber, 1952), p. 82.
12. See Langdon Gilkey, *The Shantung Compound* (New York: Harper, 1966).

CHAPTER 2

1. C. S. Lewis, *Mere Christianity* (London: Fontana Press, 1955), p. 118.
2. See C. Sanders, *Introduction to Research in English Literary History* (New York: Macmillan, 1952), pp. 143ff.
3. For more of this, see my *Set Forth Your Case* (Chicago: Moody, 1971), pp. 77-84.
4. A. N. Sherwin-White, *Roman Society and Roman Law in the New Testament* (Oxford: Clarendon, 1963), pp. 172-193.
5. Edward Conze, *Buddhist Thought in India* (Ann Arbor, Michigan: U. of Michigan, 1962), p. 31.
6. Edward J. Thomas, *The Life of Buddha as Legend and History* (New York: Barnes and Noble, 1956), p. 2.
7. Lewis, pp. 52-53.
8. Thomas Arnold, cited in Wilbur M. Smith, *Therefore, Stand* (Boston: Wilde, 1945). The reader is encouraged to see Smith's extensive treatment of the evidence for the resurrection.

CHAPTER 3

1. C. S. Lewis, *A Mind Awake, An Anthology of C. S. Lewis,* ed. Clyde S. Kilby (London: Geoffrey Bless, 1968), pp. 141, 179.
2. St. Augustine, *Confessions,* Book 1, chap. 1.
3. Wilbur M. Smith, *Therefore, Stand* (Boston: Wilde, 1945), p. 477.